EDGE BOOKS

STARS OF PRO WRESTLING

EDGE

BY JASON D. NEMETH

Consultant:
Mike Johnson, Writer
PWInsider.com

Capstone press®

Mankato, Minnesota

Edge Books are published by Capstone Press,
151 Good Counsel Drive, P.O. Box 669, Mankato, Minnesota 56002.
www.capstonepress.com
Copyright © 2010 by Capstone Press, a Capstone Publishers company.
For information regarding permission, write to Capstone Press,
151 Good Counsel Drive, P.O. Box 669, Dept. R,
Mankato, Minnesota 56002.
Printed in the United States of America in Stevens Point, Wisconsin.
022010
005697R

Library of Congress Cataloging-in-Publication Data
Nemeth, Jason D.
    Edge / by Jason D. Nemeth.
    p. cm. — (Edge. Stars of pro wrestling)
    Includes bibliographical references and index.
    Summary: "Describes the life and career of pro wrestler Adam
Copeland, also known as Edge" — Provided by publisher.
    ISBN 978-1-4296-3346-8 (library binding)
    1. Copeland, Adam, 1973– 2. Wrestlers — Canada — Biography. I. Title.
II. Series.
GV1196.C67N45 2010
796.812092 — dc22
[B]   2009002179

Editorial Credits
Mandy Robbins, editor; Ted Williams, designer; Jo Miller, media researcher

Photo Credits
Getty Images Inc./Gaye Gerard, cover, 21, 25; Hulton Archive/Darlene
    Hammond, 10; Jim McIsaac, 9; WireImage/Don Arnold, 5, 16, 22
Globe Photos/Allstar/Graham Whitby-Boot, 18
Newscom, 6, 15; WENN/Carrie Devorah, 13; Matthew Hynes, 23;
    Olivier Andrivon, 19; Orlando Sentinel/MCT/Jacob Langston, 26
Shutterstock/George Koroneos, 29
Zuma Press/Mary Ann Owen, 17

Design Elements
Shutterstock/amlet; Henning Janos; J. Danny; kzww

TABLE OF CONTENTS

Chapter 1

A LITTLE TLC

The World Heavyweight Championship belt hung high above the ring. Edge and Undertaker were facing off in a **Tables, Ladders, and Chairs (TLC) match**. Whoever reached the belt first would be the champion.

Undertaker started out strong. He hit Edge in the stomach, choked him, and twisted his arm. Then Undertaker grabbed a ladder and hit Edge with that too.

Undertaker dragged Edge partway off the side of the ring and tried to give him a *leg drop*. But Edge grabbed a chair and smashed it into Undertaker's knee. He hit Undertaker with the chair two more times. While Undertaker was dazed, Edge rolled him onto a table and dove on top of him. Both men crashed through the table.

TLC match — a match in which wrestlers use tables, ladders, and chairs as weapons

TLC matches are Edge's specialty.
He has only lost one TLC match in
his entire career.

WRESTLING MOVE

leg drop — a wrestler jumps into the air and lands with
his thigh on the opponent's head or chest

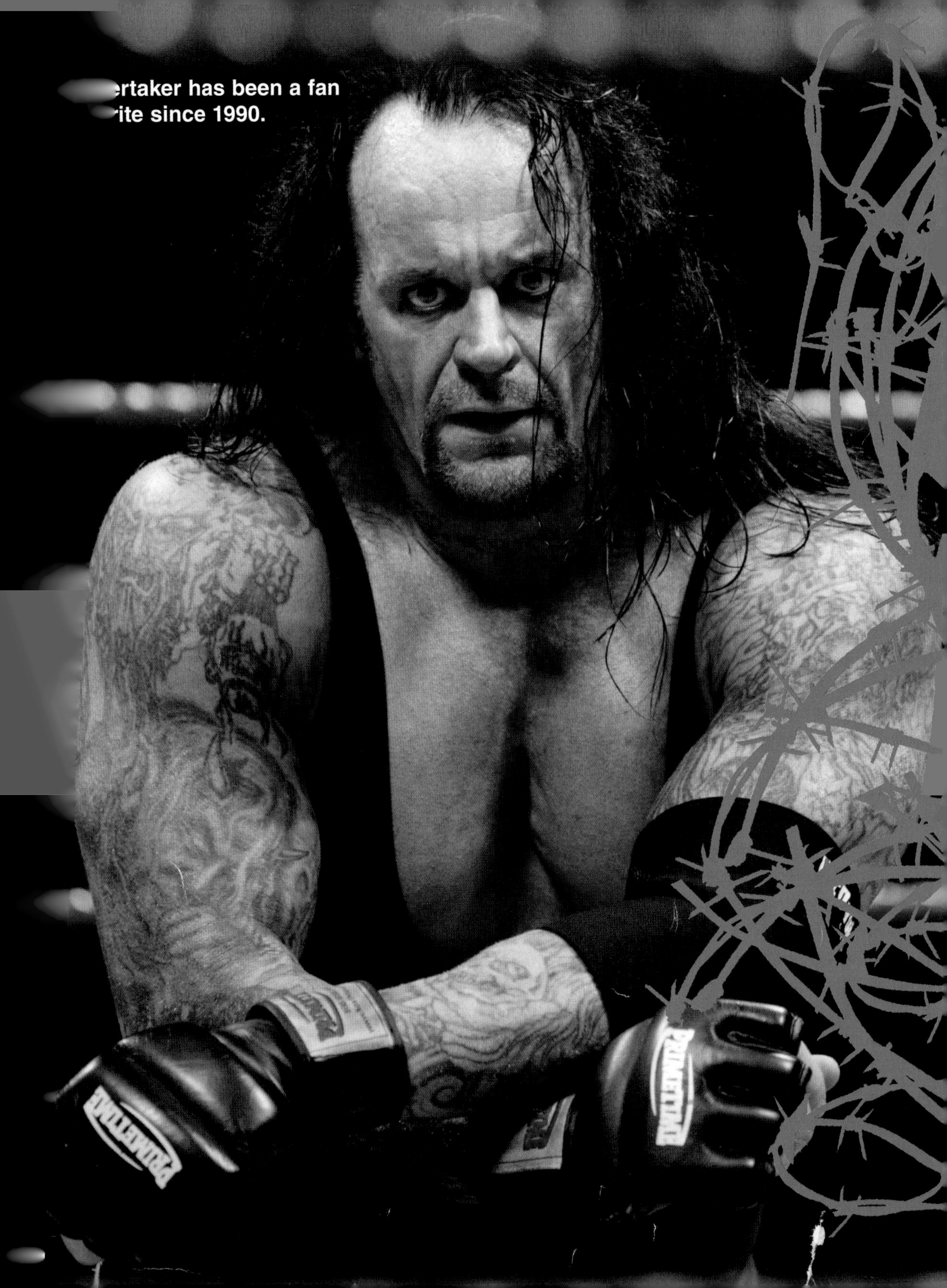

ertaker has been a fan
rite since 1990.

Edge continued his attack. He wedged Undertaker's leg between the sides of the ladder. Then he slammed the ladder shut again and again, injuring Undertaker's leg.

But Edge had underestimated Undertaker. Undertaker got up and slammed Edge onto a ladder outside the ring. It knocked the wind out of Edge, and he lay still. Undertaker set up a ladder below the belt and started to hop up it on his good leg. It looked like he would reach the belt first.

Suddenly, two of Edge's friends from the group La Familia entered the ring. They pulled Undertaker off the ladder and pounded on him. Undertaker fought them off and started to climb again. Two more wrestlers joined the fight against Undertaker. They tried to sandwich him between two chairs. But Undertaker ducked, and they hit each other. Undertaker then grabbed a chair and knocked out both of them.

With no one left to stop him, Undertaker began climbing the ladder once again. It looked like the World Heavyweight Championship was out of Edge's reach.

Chapter 2

CANADIAN SON

Adam Copeland was born on October 30, 1973, in Orangeville, Ontario, Canada. His mother, Judy Copeland, raised him while working two jobs. Adam spent a lot of time with his uncles, aunts, and grandparents. Adam's favorite uncle was Gary. Only nine years older than Adam, Uncle Gary was like a big brother.

Growing up, Adam liked action. His favorite sport was hockey. He loved the rock band KISS. He also enjoyed comic books. Once, Adam flipped off of a table and sprained his neck pretending to be Spiderman.

At home, Adam was wild and energetic. But in school, he was quiet and shy. Adam had a hard time making friends.

Adam loves watching hockey. His favorite team is the New Jersey Devils.

Most wrestling fans consider Hulk Hogan to be the first superstar of professional wrestling.

FAMILY TRAGEDY

When Adam was nine years old, his uncle Gary was in a car accident. Gary died from his injuries. Adam was heartbroken.

No one could replace Uncle Gary. But when Adam saw Hulk Hogan on TV, he knew he had found a new role model.

Adam soaked up all the wrestling he could find. He read wrestling magazines. He and his mom made popcorn and watched wrestling on TV.

SHARING A DREAM

Adam's love of wrestling also helped him make new friends at school. Jay Reso moved to Orangeville while Adam was in middle school. Jay was another wrestling fan. Adam and Jay quickly became friends. The boys helped set up the ring when wrestling matches came to Orangeville. They also traveled to Toronto to watch their favorite wrestlers compete at the Maple Leaf Gardens.

In high school, Adam and Jay met other wrestling fans. They formed a group called the Getalong Gang. The "Gang" went to the gym together every day. They wanted to get in shape so they could wrestle.

When Adam was 18, he entered an essay contest held by *The Toronto Star* newspaper. First prize was free wrestling training with professional wrestlers Ron Hutchinson and "Sweet Daddy" Siki. Adam wrote about why he wanted to be a professional wrestler. His essay won.

PAYING HIS DUES

Adam's first match was on July 1, 1992. He lost, but he wasn't discouraged. Becoming a professional wrestler was difficult. Adam had a long way to go.

But first, he had to pay the bills. Adam held many different jobs and eventually decided to go to college.

WRESTLING FACT

Before he became Edge, Adam wrestled under the names Adam Impact and Sexton Hardcastle.

When Adam wasn't at work or school, he was wrestling. He didn't make much money, and some matches were far away. For one match, he drove more than 20 hours through snow, in bitterly cold temperatures. Adam wrote about these adventures in his journals. It was a difficult time, but Adam did what he had to do to gain experience and get noticed.

Since the beginning of his career, Adam has been an intense wrestler who holds nothing back.

Chapter 3

THE PAYOFF

In 1996, Adam's hard work began to pay off. He was asked to wrestle in a World Wrestling Federation (WWF) match. The WWF is now World Wrestling Entertainment (WWE).

Eventually, Bret "The Hitman" Hart saw Adam wrestle. Hart put in a good word for Adam with the WWF. In 1997, Adam got a **developmental contract** with the WWF. This meant he had a weekly paycheck. But it didn't mean he'd be on TV.

Adam wrestled in Canada and Japan during this time. Eventually, he was called by the WWF to take another training course. Adam did his best to impress them. It worked! The WWF offered him a five-year contract and gave him his wrestling name: Edge.

developmental contract — a deal to compete in a smaller league as a way to train for a bigger league like WWE

The announcers called Edge a tortured soul when he made his WWF debut.

TAG TEAM WRESTLER

In his early career, Edge was a **tag team** wrestler. Edge's partner was his childhood friend Jay Reso. Jay's wrestling name was Christian. Together, Edge and Christian won seven Tag Team Championships.

Edge and Christian were **heels**. They **feuded** with the Hardy Boyz and the Dudley Boyz. These teams often competed in ladder matches. Ladder matches were like TLC matches, but without the tables and chairs.

Edge developed an exciting in-ring personality while he was a tag team wrestler.

Christian was smaller than a lot of other wrestlers, but he packed a big punch.

tag team — when two wrestlers partner together against other teams

heel — a wrestler who acts as a villain in the ring

feud — to argue and fight with another person or group of people

WRESTLING FACT

Edge has won 12 Tag Team titles. Seven of those times, he was paired with Christian.

Making His Own Way

In 2001, Edge and Christian started to feud. Their tag team broke up. Edge set out to prove that he could be a champion on his own. He won the Intercontinental Championship three times in 2001. He also won the United States Championship.

After many singles matches, Edge teamed up with other wrestlers again. He won two more Tag Team Championships. For one match, he teamed up with his childhood hero, Hulk Hogan. He won another title with Rey Mysterio Jr.

Teaming up with Hogan was a dream come true for Edge.

Edge and Rey Mysterio Jr. (pictured) defeated Kurt Angle and Chris Benoit for the WWE Tag Team Championship.

OUT OF THE RING

In 2003, Edge's neck began to hurt. But wrestlers are used to living in pain. Edge waited two months before he saw a doctor. The doctor said he needed to rest and let his neck heal. Edge ignored the doctor's advice and kept wrestling. After two more months, Edge had to stop wrestling. He had broken his neck. Two disks in his spine were broken. If there had been three broken disks, his career would have been over. Edge had surgery. He stopped wrestling for a year to heal.

Edge had lots of time to think while his neck was healing. He started looking at his old journals. He decided to put them together to make a book. Edge's book was called *Adam Copeland On Edge*. It tells Adam's story from birth to the time of his neck injury.

WRESTLING FACT

Edge had a small part in the movie *Highlander: Endgame*. His character in the movie was also called Edge.

Edge's Injuries

Edge's aggressive wrestling style has taken a toll on his body. Edge had surgery for a broken neck in 2003. The next year, he sprained his ankle. Soon after, Edge broke his left hand. He continued wrestling wearing a cast. Edge injured a tendon in his chest in July 2007. He had to give up his World Heavyweight belt and take five months off to heal. Edge has also hurt his shoulder several times, and he has had steel rods placed in all of his teeth.

MAN ON A MISSION

Edge started wrestling again in 2004. He set his sights on the two titles he had never won: the WWE Championship and the World Heavyweight Championship.

At WrestleMania in 2005, Edge beat five wrestlers to win a Money in the Bank match. This meant that he could cash in his win for a shot at the WWE Championship. At New Year's Revolution 2006, Edge defeated John Cena for the title.

Edge feuded with John Cena for most of 2006.

Edge's cocky attitude has made him one of the most popular heels in WWE.

WRESTLING FACT

In his high school yearbook, Adam Copeland was voted "Most Likely to Win the WWF Championship."

Chapter 4

CHAMPIONSHIP GOLD

In 2007, Edge went after the World Heavyweight Championship. It was currently held by Undertaker. The two men battled for over a year. The belt went back and forth between them.

Their feud came to an exciting head at One Night Stand 2008 in a TLC match. Undertaker proved hard to defeat. He knocked Edge out of the ring and started climbing the ladder. Edge's friends tried to help him out, but they couldn't defeat Undertaker. It seemed Edge might not get the championship belt back after all.

The distractions from his friends gave Edge time to recover. When Undertaker was almost to the top of the ladder, Edge dove into the ring. He pushed over the ladder. Undertaker crashed through four tables set up outside the ring. Edge picked up the ladder and quickly climbed to the belt. He was the new World Heavyweight Champion.

Edge won the World Heavyweight Championship for the first time on May 11, 2007.

Undertaker and Edge had lots of brutal matches during their feud.

Undertaker came back for revenge in 2008. A cell match was set up for SummerSlam later that year. In this type of match, the entire ring area is enclosed in a cage, and there are no rules. The only way to win is for one wrestler to knock out his opponent for a count of 10.

Edge and Undertaker traded punches and kicks. They hit each other with chairs and TV monitors from outside the ring. Finally, Undertaker gave Edge the *Tombstone Piledriver*. Edge was out cold. Then Undertaker carried Edge up onto a ladder and chokeslammed him down from the top. Edge went straight through the mat. Fire shot up out of the hole.

WRESTLING MOVE

Tombstone Piledriver — a wrestler turns his opponent upside down and then drops into a kneeling position, driving the opponent's head into the mat

BACK FROM THE EDGE

Edge was not seen or heard from for more than three months. Finally, at Survivor Series 2008, Edge reappeared. He took the place of Jeff Hardy in a three-way match against Triple H and Vladimir Kozlov. Just after the match started, Jeff Hardy suddenly appeared. He grabbed a steel chair and tried to knock out Edge for taking his place.

Instead of hitting Edge, Hardy accidentally knocked out both Triple H and Kozlov. Edge tackled Hardy and knocked him out. Then Edge pinned Triple H for the win. He was once again the WWE Champion.

WHAT THE FUTURE HOLDS

Who knows what Edge will do now that he's won all the belts? Perhaps he'll try to win them more times than anyone else has.

Edge once said that he would like to write another book. He would also like to star in a superhero movie. Whatever Edge's goals are, he won't quit working until he meets them. That's how he makes his dreams come true.

Edge showed off his World Heavyweight Championship belt before losing it to Undertaker at WrestleMania in March, 2008.

GLOSSARY ★ ★ ★ ★ ★

developmental contract (duh-VEHL-up-ment-uhl KAHN-tract) — a deal in which a wrestler is paid to compete in a smaller league as a way to train for a bigger league like WWE

feud (FYOOD) — to participate in a long-running quarrel between two people or groups of people

heel (HEEL) — a wrestler who acts as a villain in the ring

tag team (TAG TEEM) — when two wrestlers partner together against other teams

tendon (TEN-duhn) — a strong band of tissue that joins a muscle to a bone

TLC match (TEE EL SEE MACH) — TLC stands for tables, ladders, and chairs; in this match, all these items can be used as weapons, and a ladder is needed to reach the prize hung high above the ring.

READ MORE

Kaelberer, Angie Peterson. *Hulk Hogan: Pro Wrestler Terry Bollea.* Pro Wrestlers. Mankato, Minn.: Capstone Press, 2004.

Schaefer, A. R. *The Undertaker: Pro Wrestler Mark Callaway.* Pro Wrestlers. Mankato, Minn.: Capstone Press, 2003.

Shields, Brian, and Kevin Sullivan. *WWE Encyclopedia.* New York: DK Publishing, 2009.

INTERNET SITES

FactHound offers a safe, fun way to find Internet sites related to this book. All of the sites on FactHound have been researched by our staff.

Here's all you do:

Visit *www.facthound.com*

FactHound will fetch the best sites for you!

INDEX ★ ★ ★ ★ ★ ★ ★